AFRODESCENDANT

Blackmen Must Provide for AFRODESCENDANT People First

A & A Ziyad

Foreword

Today, an overarching predicament of almost all Afrodescendants has affected our potential and capability to survive and thrive in the world - one where we are disregarded, oppressed, and suppressed because we don't have a nationality that unites Black people who are descendants of the transatlantic slave trade. We are called many things – we are negro, colored, Black American, and others that are merely degrading. The most prevalent now is the term "African American," which we are not!

African American are people who,

1. are born in Africa: even if they are Black, White, Indian, Chinese, or any race,

2. come to the USA or the Americas to become a citizen,

3. know their language, culture, and religion,

4. know their identity, heritage, and history,

5. when they become a citizen of the USA, they are called African Americans,

For example, an individual white person born in Africa who later becomes a citizen in the USA or any country in the Americas is called African American because they were born in Africa. The commonly held belief that all Black people in the Americas are the descendants of the Africans brought through the transatlantic slave trade is incorrect.

In 2002, Black leaders from 19 countries in the Americas and Caribbean convened and reached an agreement on a new identity. The new identity, termed "Afrodescendant," was officially recognized and documented in the United Nations in 2006. As a result, it established a distinct international political identity for us, over 300,000,000 people who are descendants of the Transatlantic slave trade in the Americas.

Afrodescendants are people whose forefathers:

1. were forcibly dispossessed of their homeland, Africa:

2. were transported to the Americas and Slavery Diaspora for the purpose of enslavement:

3. were subjected to plantation slavery:

4. were subjected to forced mixed breeding and rape;

5. have experienced, through force, the loss of mother tongue, culture, and religion; and/or

6. have experienced racial discrimination due to lost ties or partially lost ties from their original identity.

Before this revolutionary change in 2006, we were not acknowledged as human beings with inherent human rights in the Americas and Europe. We were seen as slaves and now descendants of slaves, scattered and oppressed and not in possession of our human rights. This brought official recognition to us, and we are now recognized as a new nation of people.

Thank you, Silis Muhammad (CEO of the Lost-Found Nation of Islam) and the Black leaders from 19 countries, for your strength in your stand!

Contents

Chapter 1: Ancestor Provided after Slavery

Throughout history, Black people and our ancestors have demonstrated remarkable self-determination and resilience in the face of oppression and discrimination. Despite being subjected to slavery, segregation, forced assimilation[1], and other forms of systemic racism, our ancestors consistently fought for their rights and dignity.

But today, in this fast-paced world, not only do we, Afrodescendants, still face dehumanization and ethnocide[2] to stop our self-determination by Caucasian governments, but also the scarcity of economics, education, and motivation to unite as one people. However, what happened to the

---

[1] Forced assimilation is the process of compelling individuals or groups to adopt another group's culture, language, customs, and norms through coercion, oppression, outright imposition, or integration. This can occur through policies, laws, or actions imposed by a dominant group onto a marginalized or minority group, often aiming to homogenize society or exert control. Force assimilation can have significant social, psychological, and cultural impacts on the affected populations, leading to feelings of alienation, loss of identity, and resistance. https://law.adelaide.edu.au/ua/media/573/ch4-alr-35-2-pruim.pdf

[2] Ethnocide refers to the deliberate and systematic destruction of the culture, language, identity, and way of life of a particular ethnic group. It often involves efforts to eradicate or suppress cultural practices, traditions, and beliefs, as well as the imposition of the dominant culture onto the targeted group. Ethnocide can occur through various means, including forced assimilation, cultural repression, displacement, and violence. It is a form of cultural genocide that aims to eliminate the distinctiveness and autonomy of an ethnic group. What is Ethnocide? https://www.americanbar.org/groups/human_rights/dignity-rights-initiative/ethnocide-project/what-is-ethnocide-/

determination and motivation to fight that we are known for?

What Have We and Our Ancestors Not Faced?

Black people have endured centuries of racism, violence, and discrimination, including the terror of the KKK, the brutalities of slavery, and the culture of systemic hate from Caucasian societies. Despite this, our African ancestors who came out of slavery persevered and fought for equality, justice, and dignity.

The Ku Klux Klan (KKK) is a white supremacist group that was founded in the aftermath of the American Civil War. The group aimed to maintain white supremacy and terrorize our ancestors, who wanted to keep our forefathers under their way of life as a servant. The KKK used violence, intimidation, and acts of terrorism, including lynchings and other violence against them, to maintain their dominance and control.

Slavery was a system of forced labor in the United States government before the Civil War. Under slavery, our ancestors were considered property and were subjected to brutal treatment, including physical, sexual, and mental abuse, lack of medical care, and limited access to education and basic rights. Slavery was abolished with the passage of the 13th Amendment to the Constitution in 1865, but our ancestors and Black people today continue to face discrimination and racism in the decades that followed.

Neo-Nazis and the KKK are individuals and groups who adhere to a white nationalist ideology and seek to create a white society where people of different races are inferior to white people. The different races live in these white societies to help maintain it, while white people have superior status and power. White nationalist supremacy groups like the Neo-Nazis, the KKK, and individuals have been responsible for acts of violence and terrorism against minority groups, including our ancestors, in the United States and other countries.

But, the most important thing that we don't remember today in these white societies is the fact that our ancestors were captured and brought to these countries as forced laborers to build and maintain these societies. Some of us are on these airlines' manufacturing, retail, and CEO jobs right now. Working for who? Whose society or economy and most of all, whose way of life is being maintained? Is it the Blackman's and the Black woman's way of life or economy, or is it the White man's and White woman's life and economy? In fact, we don't have a way of life. Always remember that our ancestors wanted to be free, be independent, and build their own. We heard our grandparents say God blesses the child that has its own, but the meaning today should be that God blesses those people who have their own. Black men and women need to rise up to the occasion to establish a government that protects themselves.

However, it seems we have forgotten our original ways – to fight, retaliate, and stand up against these white societies and white supremacist groups. Our ancestors, in marked contrast, used to fight for their rights. However, we, the Afrodescendants, seem to have accepted our fates. Why is this so? This is because of these categorizations as nonconformists, deviants, criminals, and lazy, along with blatant criminal aggressions on us, which have taken a toll on our self-worth and determination.

Statistically, the above statement is more than evident. Economically, Afrodescendants are one of the major minority groups willing to work but are unemployed. Black men who receive less income and acquire only one-third of what their white coworkers make lead to a domino effect where less income turns into less saving, and less money leads to substandard education, unsatisfactory resources, and poor health.

This disparity is also seen in education due to the lack of economic resources for predominately Black schools. The Black way of life, created by white supremacist institutions, manifested in the U.S. education system that fosters an atmosphere of despair, poverty, and uncertainty. The U.S. education system is aimed at affecting the education of young Black individuals, where Black students find it systematically hard to perform well, and their education is hindered by the way they are stereotyped and outcasted. For example, the school-to-prison pipeline causes long-term economic disparity in the Black community. Black history and books are taken out of the schools, and libraries are being replaced with detention centers. Because of these systems, schools are not able to perform at the expected level and are being shut down.

Similarly, the Afrodescendants' family life and culture are also being targeted. Honestly speaking, it is the most imperative to repair and protect our heritage and culture, mainly due to the side effects of slavery and ongoing physical and psychological attacks on Black communities. This does not only revolve around the high percentage of single parenthood, poverty, and emotional unavailability but also involves the purpose of Black people working as a nation of people, which has been lost.

But why?

The part of our Afrodescendants' lives that is frequently ignored is our life's course. When we perform badly, the simple answer is to work harder, e.g., "If you don't want to suffer, stop suffering." Pull yourself up by your bootstraps. Such hollow responses to define our obstacles are not only a driving force of our failure but also the pinnacle of the problem we have to confront daily. It is said to pull yourself up by your bootstrap, but you cannot do that when your boots are taken! The fact is, Black people suffer regardless of the field or stage of their lives, not because of our intrinsic values but owing to the external white values that affect ours. White privilege and majority advantage are not just opinions, myths, or legends but well-established and profound realities. In a world where people are given clear benefits because of their race, how are we, the so-called "inferior color," supposed to survive? This helps white people's way of life to hinder Black people's way of life.

We fail today because we succumb to our little shells that rob us of our ability to bloom into something more. We aren't given the right to the resources we need because the whites have our lives pre-designed for us, even though our lives do not belong to them.

Let us change the curriculum, change the representation, change the job opportunities by creating jobs for ourselves, and let's see ourselves thrive. Let's think about this theory differently. A Black child born into a socioeconomic nuclear family because his parents aren't taken away for slavery or other manual labor work and have their own nation, attends a private school where the curriculum appreciates and recognizes Black role models and politicians, where the Black school's curriculum does not negate his rich history; where Black teachers acknowledge and help the student, without systematic racism, so he can graduate with a standard diploma and start and create businesses. And where he is not considered less because he is Black and is able to provide for his society. If this happens, only then can we expect him to succeed.

The unfortunate reality is that the above example is just hypothetical. Racism has been passed down from generation to generation, rooted everywhere: in education, criminal justice, financial departments, health care, employment, housing, media, politics, and whatnot.

Today, we Black people of all ages face this systematic and mental abuse, but some of us don't even recognize these disparities anymore. But these complications have driven us away from what is needed. They have taken away our self-determination and the community we once had. They have taken away our determination to fight together, act as a nation of people, and thrive as a community. Our ancestors had them, and they won. If we want to win again, this is the only way – the last resort.

Our Role Is to Provide

Because of this impediment we face today, we have

become dependent on them and resorted to immediate gratification rather than long-term goals. It has led us to distance away from our natural aptitude, which is to provide for our people first. A Blackman must be able to provide for his family, neighborhood, community, and nation of people at large.

Let's observe the other races, e.g., the Arabs, Asians, Europeans, and Indians of India. The men in these societies provide without going to other people (rich man's table, US Government) to solve all their problems. They don't have to look outside for help; they have everything they need to provide for their society, community, and family. These communities have developed manufacturing plants, factories, technology, and education catering to societal needs. Sadly, we don't see it in Afrodescendant communities because we have been robbed of our way of life, which was once ruled by camaraderie, togetherness, respect and mutual support.

These other nations produce food, clothing, and shelter for their people; they deliver healthy food and develop jobs that maintain their way of life. They maintain their economies, whereas the Black economy only faces a downfall. This is because the Caucasian system systematically programs us to find jobs in their society and be satisfied with what minimum we get. Having a job is essential, but creating your own businesses will maintain an economic system among our people. The motivation of being independent keeps us from having to swerve through obstacles in someone else's economy.

We have to start from the origin: the unit of all life — family. Not only does a man need to be the provider of the family, providing for his children's and wife's needs, but he also needs to be emotionally present as he teaches and guides his family on how to be successful in life. If you are resilient, you will make your children resilient. You will teach them how life works when you live it.

Once you're done, move on to your neighborhood and community to help your nation, the Afrodescendant people. Provide for your community by launching business ventures that create jobs to provide food, clothes, and shelter, help the ones in need, provide for those who cannot fend for themselves, as well as those who have lost hope. To help create a strong economic system for your nation of people, you have to help them gain hope and self-determination and think of being independent. You have to be there for each other.

How Our Ancestors Dealt with Racist Societies

Even though our ancestors faced the same issues we are facing today, they successfully dealt with them through self-determination and perseverance.

When the Emancipation Proclamation by Abraham Lincoln freed us by executive order, were we really free? Did the plight of the Black community end there? No, they still fought on! Because they knew they deserved a lot more and had the resilience to achieve that, too.

We, Afrodescendants, today have an identity that our forefathers did not have coming out of slavery. However, we are treated the same way. They weren't allowed to enter mainstream America and did not have civil or human rights or a government identification. So, they did the only thing they could do: rely on each other. Before the Civil Rights Act was enacted, Black and White people were separated. Black people were building – they built their own banks, schools, factories, farms, newspapers, insurance companies, pharmaceuticals, and everything necessary. They were progressing despite not being allowed to enter mainstream America.

Here are some notable examples of their progress:

Political Representation: During the Reconstruction era after the Civil War, our ancestors were in politics and held elected offices at the local, state, and federal levels. For example, Hiram Revels became the first Black man to serve in the US Senate in 1870, and Blanche K. Bruce served in the Senate from 1875 to 1881. Similarly, many Black people were elected to state legislatures and held other political positions during this time. This demonstrates we can govern ourselves. Then came the KKK and black codes.

Education

The establishment of Historically Black Colleges And Universities (HBCUs) during this period gave Black people higher education opportunities. Our ancestors founded institutions such as Howard University, Tuskegee Institute, University of Islam Fisk University, and many other colleges and universities to provide educational opportunities for Black people previously denied access. These institutions produced many notable graduates who became leaders in various fields.

Business and Entrepreneurship

Despite facing significant barriers and discrimination, our ancestors were able to start and run successful businesses. Notable examples include Madam C.J. Walker, one of the first self-made female millionaires in the United States through her hair care and beauty products company, and Robert Church Sr., one of the wealthiest Black men in the South through his various business ventures. Golden State Mutual Life Insurance company, by George A. Beavers Jr. and Norman O. Houston, had assets of $56,046,360.58 in

1944. Marcus Garvey had a fleet of cargo-ships going coast to coast, trading with Black businesses worldwide. The Most Honorable Elijah Muhammad said, "We are a nation. We do business with the governments," and negotiated with Peru's government to import millions of tons of fish to create business not just for the Nation of Islam but for Black people.

Arts and Culture

The period between the end of the Civil War and the rise of the Civil Rights Movement saw the emergence of many of our notable ancestors, who were writers and musicians, inventors, engineers, and architects. The examples include Booker T. Washington, who wrote the famous autobiography "Up from Slavery," W.E.B. Du Bois, who co-founded the National Association for the Advancement of Colored People (NAACP) and wrote influential works on race relations, and musicians such as Bessie Smith, Louis Armstrong, and Duke Ellington, who helped to shape the development of music industry.

To aid our people, many individuals stood up, like Malcolm X, Martin Luther King, and other prominent figures who exhibited solidarity and resilience.

Malcolm X worked tirelessly to improve the lives of Black people in the United States. He contributed to the struggle for racial justice by advocating for Black

Nationalism, emphasizing the importance of having a nation of your own, a distinct Black identity, culture, and political movement. He believed that Black people should control their communities and institutions and not depend on white society for advancement. He also promoted self-determination. Malcolm X believed that Black people needed to take control of their destinies rather than rely on white society for their advancement. He encouraged Black people to educate themselves and become economically self-sufficient and criticized the idea of integration as a way to achieve equality. He fought against racism as a vocal critic of the systemic racism and discrimination faced by Black people in all aspects of life. He spoke out against police brutality, unequal access to education and employment opportunities, and the many other forms of discrimination that Black people experienced. He advocated building your own schooling system and creating employment opportunities by building your own businesses. He learned all of this from the (peace be upon him) Most Honorable Elijah Muhammad. Do for yourself, meaning for your people and nation.

Our predecessors fought for their education and became journalists, nurses, factory owners, landlords, and millionaires. They created banks, trust funds, insurance, and communities, towns, and cities. They built all that was needed by themselves as a community. They even dealt with public transport segregation and the consequences of not adhering to the rules that resulted in women being jailed. They led the Montgomery Bus Boycott. They refused to use any transport on Mondays and skipped school, work, and other activities because it mattered how their community was treated. They did not want any of their community members to face oppression, so they stood together and put an end to the segregated public transport. In 1963, King organized the historic March on Washington for jobs and freedom, which drew over 200,000 people to the National Mall in Washington, DC. There, King delivered his famous "I Have a Dream" speech, which called for an end to racism and discrimination in the United States.

Many campaigns, movements, and leaders stood up and got exactly what they wanted—not the life designed or needed by the white folks, but what they wanted their lives to look like.

Unfortunately, the white supremacists did not like their success, and just like they do now, they attempted to tear down our achievements. As Martin Luther King said after his historic 'I Have A Dream' speech, "the dream became a nightmare." After the Civil Rights Bill passed, he stated that he led his people into a burning house, meaning we, as Black people, should be looking to become separate as self-determined people, not integrated. We integrated into their way of life. Ethnocide was done and is still happening to us. Why critical race theory is a big issue for white people?

Like in the 1900s, they began the Red Summer. During the Red Summer, there were numerous incidents of white mobs attacking Black cities, towns, communities, and individuals, often with local authorities' implicit or explicit approval. Some of the most notorious examples of this violence occurred in cities such as Chicago, Washington, DC, and Tulsa, Oklahoma.

In Chicago, a white man named Eugene Williams killed a young Blackman while swimming in Lake Michigan. The ensuing riots resulted in the deaths of 38 people, the majority of whom were Black. In Washington, DC, violence erupted after a white woman accused a Blackman of assaulting her. The ensuing riots lasted for four days and resulted in the deaths of 15 people.

The most infamous incident occurred in Tulsa, Oklahoma, where a white mob attacked and destroyed a wealthy Black community known as "Black Wall Street." The mob killed an estimated 300 Black residents and destroyed more than 1,000 homes and businesses. Hundreds of more Black towns and cities were burned down and flooded to become lakes.

They even passed certain policies and warrants in the 1950s to build highways and freeways in major

Black-populated cities. One of the most significant of these policies was the Federal-Aid Highway Act of 1956, which provided funding for constructing the Interstate Highway System. This massive infrastructure project was intended to connect cities and promote economic growth, but it often came at the expense of Black communities.

In many cases, the construction of highways and freeways involved the demolition of entire communities, displacing thousands of residents and destroying businesses and community institutions. Black neighborhoods were often targeted for destruction because they were successful, self-sustaining communities seen as less valuable than white neighborhoods and were located in areas that were considered suitable for highway construction.

Furthermore, highway construction often reinforced segregation patterns by dividing communities and creating physical barriers between Black and White neighborhoods. This made it more difficult for Black residents to access jobs, education, and other resources that white neighborhoods had while Black resources were being destroyed.

Another policy that contributed to the displacement of Black communities was the Urban Renewal program, which was initiated in the 1950s and continued throughout the 1960s. This program was intended to revitalize blighted urban areas. Still, it often involved the demolition of entire neighborhoods and the displacement of thousands of residents, many of whom were Black ancestors' communities. The impact of these policies on our ancestors was devastating. Countless families were forced to leave their homes and communities, often with little or no compensation. Entire neighborhoods were destroyed, erasing generations of history, economic wealth, and culture. This forced them to look outside their community for jobs.

Not only that, they started blaming Black people for drug issues, crimes, or anything bad that happened in the United States. The Narcotics operations by the CIA and police departments in the 1970s targeted the Black community with drugs to finance their international operations, called the War on Drugs. The Highway Act and the Renewal Acts redlining forced poverty and caused desperate times. This resulted in the selling and offering of drugs, which increased drug usage, health issues, and incarceration numbers, destructing the communities' lifestyles and stereotyping us.

This discrimination, oppression, and even stereotyping followed them throughout their lives. But they fought it with self-determination, unity, and solidarity.

Due to the Caucasian educational system having a heavy influence on Black people, we have forgotten our way of life. We have resorted to dependence and complacency, leading to a myriad of problems we face today, forgetting our strength as a community.

Afrodescendants have become lost from freedom, independence, and self-determination. Hopefully, the realization of providing for our people despite the white power structure will seep into our mindset. This will catalyze us to explore our rich history and empower role models who will teach us how to live and prosper in the world of visible and invisible economic and psychological war upon us, the Afrodescendants.[3]

---

[3] We, the Blackman, must provide for our people first. We have always integrated with people and helped others even when we were hurting the most. We must stop that and have our best interests at heart. Take care of us first, then help others.

Chapter 2: The American Government Uses Psychological Warfare Through Education

In the present day, the effects of slavery are still apparent. The roots of the wide socioeconomic disparities that so-called African Americans (Afrodescendants) face today can be traced back to the age of slavery. It is imperative to understand slavery's history to understand the world today. The scars of slavery are visible in the present system in the form of mass imprisonment, police violence, and a denial of educational opportunities. Education regarding slavery was critical in the early 1900s, and now, in 2023, the State Department of Education and the Federal Department of Education are violating Black children's human rights to education by keeping their history from them because it offends white students. This is taxation without representation in the school system.

American slavery and the Jim Crow era are not being taught in the schools of America. Educators do not pay heed to the issue, and textbooks do not have enough material on these issues. Therefore, students are unaware of the significant role slavery played in shaping the United States. Moreover, they also do not know the impact it continues to have on race relations in America.

The textbooks include the history of the Civil War but tend to omit the perspective of enslaved people. Black people's history is taught from a narrative of despair, struggle, and hardship. Because of how it is taught, Afrodescendant students tend to have a negative view of their history and thus have no sense or realization of their ancestors' accomplishments and achievements.

The US government doesn't want Blacks to know their history. After getting released from slavery, Black people built cities, towns, and manufacturing companies for themselves. They started building an economic structure among themselves. However, the American system will not highlight these achievements. They don't want to teach what happened from 1865 to 1955—when we Black people achieved certain goals for ourselves that have an impact on how we see the world today. For example, Madam Walker invented the hot comb so that Black women could wear different hairstyles. This invention has led to other similar inventions, such as the flat iron, so what we do impacts the world like rap music is today.

If one delves into Black history from the prism of research, one will learn what they did and their achievements and accomplishments. Moreover, one will also realize how the American colonizers destroyed everything that the Afrodescendants' ancestors did for themselves. The colonizers captured our ancestors from Africa to build a society and a way of life for the colonizers in the Americas. This was the first way they exploited us, the Black people. The second was depriving us of our history and languages, so we could not talk to one another in our mother tongue. Your mother tongue connects you to your heritage and helps you acquire the knowledge of yourself. Now you are cut off from your history because you don't know your ancestors' language who were captured from Africa and Arabia.

People should not be controlled. They should be taught about their history; they should be told who they are, what they are, and what they have done. You cannot control them when they have the knowledge of themselves, knowing who they truly are. They tell students what happened during physical slavery but don't inform them about the psychological and biological repercussions of slavery. They fabricate the knowledge because they don't want them to know their history. The point white people want is not to narrate American history as a chronicle of oppression and shame but to describe American history as a story of power and great achievements. Slavery has much to do with the making of the United States, and everyone should be aware of the erroneous past.

Enslaved Black people of many cultures who created and built colonizers' worlds. However, they are shown as the brutalized victims of over four hundred years of oppression. People don't know they had much to do with remaking the United States during its rebound reconstruction in the 1860s to 1880s.

The American textbooks do not highlight history as they should have been. In 1863, Abraham Lincoln's emancipation proclamation announced that all enslaved people held in the states would be set free. However, the schoolteachers do not provide a detailed explanation of the proclamation. Moreover, the curriculum taught in American schools and universities generally adheres to white perspectives. It does give basic information about Abraham Lincoln and the end of slavery, but the curriculum evades discussing them in great detail. In the school curriculum, there is no discussion of Black people in the chapters on the history of reconstruction after the Civil War, as the pages simply jump from Abraham Lincoln to civil rights. As history suggests, white Americans did not help them; instead, they only did aggravate their grievances during and after the Civil War. This is when Black people struggled a lot. Abraham Lincoln, in 1862, told a few free black men that Congress set aside a sum of money to establish a negro colony because white people would not want black people to have equal freedom. They would not want black people to have equality and freedom with them. Lincoln felt that the USA was a white man's nation only. However, none of this is duly mentioned or discussed in great detail in American history books.

The American Civil Rights Movement was a mass protest movement during the mid-1950s against discrimination and separate but equal. The efforts of fathers and their descendants to resist racial oppression could be seen through this movement. However, American textbooks do not provide ample information about this movement.

Martin Luther King Jr. talked about civil rights in his speeches and said that he wanted Blacks and Caucasians to have brotherly relations. Particularly in his last speeches, he emphasized the need for self-determination among Black people to govern themselves and lead their lives free of oppression, coercion, and intimidation. In the last few years of his life, Martin Luther made a special mention of having a dream, accentuating the importance of vision in pursuit of absolute freedom. However, sadly, that dream has turned out to be a nightmare, and he has led his people to a burning house. See, they don't teach that in the history books. Moreover, Martin Luther King also expressed his noble intentions to go to Washington DC on the campaign to get "our check" today we say-(reparations) - the most important phase of his struggle that couldn't find its place in the academic curriculum. However, White Americans employ his speeches merely to build a narrative that only they want to promote.

Taught to children 6 to 14 years old, the school curriculum focuses entirely on the European way of life. Schools only think of safeguarding, nurturing, and uplifting European societies because they are taught and trained in like manner. American schools are not educating students to promote Black communities and their sociocultural traditions and practices.

The Americans ruin the Afrodescendants' way of life by keeping them away from the knowledge of their own way of life and heritage. This is because those who knew about the past have taken it to their graves. The history that is taught to our children is fabricated. Schoolchildren don't learn about the achievements of Black people because these things aren't mentioned anywhere. As mentioned in the school curriculum, Europeans are always behind great inventions, such as the light bulb, car, computer, and whatnot. The truth is that European men did not invent all of these. However, Black students are not educated or taught about the history from the Black perspective, which is injustice and an utter human rights violation. As articulated by critical race theory, the laws, social and political movements, and media are shaped by race and ethnicity. In marked contrast, the school textbooks conceal and deform the true history in such a way that the entire history is altered. More's the pity our schoolchildren are taught the deformed version of history, which has less to do with reality and more with fictionalized truth. This means that the students of African descent are unaware of their true history. History gives a person the loyalty that comes from being proud of who they are and where they have come from. History depicts what a person is and what they can endure, achieve and accomplish in the long run. If we know our history, we can create our future as we want it to be.

American education system paints a false narrative that the Afrodescendants are inferior to whites and are not great people because of such ingrained inferiority and inherited subservience. By controlling, manipulating, and exploiting Black people, they can get what they want and impose their way of life on non-white races. This can be referred to as psychological warfare. The term refers to the planned use of propaganda to impact the emotions, opinions, attitudes, and behavior of opposing parties.

After the 1860s, Black people escaped slavery and built colleges and industrial units. This was done in

America during Jim Crow laws, and Black Codes were enforced. Jim Crow laws eradicated racial segregation laws, which existed for about a century, from the post-Civil War era until the 1980s. They began in 1865, following the approval of the 13th Amendment, which eradicated slavery in the United States.

These laws were meant to disregard the so-called Americans Negro by rejecting their right to vote, hold jobs, get an education, or other opportunities. Those who attempted to challenge Jim Crow laws often faced arrests, jail sentences, violence, hefty fines, and even death. Still, during this time, they managed to construct banks, factories, and cities. This shows the discrimination they were facing in their daily lives. However, educators will never inform students about this significant period of history in detail.

During this period, theaters and restaurants were separated, and public parks were forbidden for so-called American Negro to enter. Waiting rooms in bus and train stations, restrooms, building entrances, elevators, cemeteries, and water fountains were also segregated. Segregation was enforced in phone booths, public swimming pools, jails, hospitals, asylums, and residential homes for disabled and elderly citizens. In addition to that, laws prohibited so-called Negro from living in neighborhoods that they want to live in. Several other segregation-based practices speak volumes of the rampant discrimination faced by the generations of Afrodescendants. For instance, some states introduced separate textbooks for students of different races. African Americans were given other Bibles, e.g., the Negro Bible, to swear on in the courts of Atlanta. In many towns and cities, signs were posted that restricted the entry of so-called Negros, colored American or African Americans. Who are you, and who determines this identity for you?

In 1861, more than 7 million Black people were enslaved when the Civil War broke out. During this period, the Black Codes were imposed, abolishing citizens' voting rights. These codes further widened the disparity among citizens, as Black offenders typically received longer sentences than white people. However, as mentioned in the academic curriculum, American history is silent on these issues. Knowing about one's history is a child's basic, fundamental right. The children must be educated in their mother tongue first and know their history before anything else. According to the research carried out by the United Nations. Children who learn about themselves, their language, and history don't become violent because they respect and value themselves. So, when they look at other human beings, they treat them as they see themselves.

It was also mentioned in the research that one of the reasons why Black people are so frustrated and self-sabotaging is because they receive European education. Thus, their way of life is heavily influenced by European schools of thought. Black people deserve the right to be educated according to their way of life and how they see it going to benefit their people in the country or state that they live in. Acquiring basic education, such as reading, writing, and solving arithmetic problems, is insufficient.

We are at a crossroads of history. We must decide and act wisely so that we do not keep treading on the same path as the previous generation did, and we must educate our children to put an end to the ongoing psychological war launched against our children and the Afrodescendant people's origin. The questions that should be asked are: Does the United States educational system cater to all people's needs? If it works for everyone, why can't its positive results be seen? Is there a possibility of some people failing and the rest succeeding, despite being the beneficiaries of the same educational system?

Bridging the equality divide requires both reconciliation and truth. To tell the truth, teachers must have adequate knowledge about the history of Afrodescendant people. The last few decades have seen a phenomenal rise in new research studies focusing on Afrodescendants' history. Unfortunately, some new information and findings rarely find their way into textbooks.

Some people say to reduce racial differences, candid conversations about the nature of white privilege should be encouraged. People should talk about how white privilege still prevails despite reconstruction, the civil rights movement, and freedom. Ultimately, teaching the truth about slavery will only be a very small step in the right direction, but it is indeed crucial. Suppose educational institutions don't know about our country's early history. In that case, they are unlikely to develop feasible solutions to bridge the increasing racial inequalities now and in the future. It is the moral responsibility of all of us to move forward toward achieving the American dream by rooting out the Willy Lynch Syndrome lingering remnants of slavery that persist in the United States. However, in the past 60 years, this has been discussed and worked on, but that has not performed as desired. Afrodescendants pay taxes in the USA education system but don't have the right to educate our children in the manner that we, the Afrodescendant people, know is best for our children to move into the future! That is denying us our self-determination and taxation without representation. Afrodescendant people must have the right to educate their children separately, stopping them from becoming Oreo cookies - black on the outside and educated from the narrative of Europeans on the inside, which is psychological warfare. You are not being educated from the Black narrative of the Black way of life, which is truthful, righteous, rich in culture, highly intelligent, and innovative up to modern times. Being educated by our way of life shall stop us from depending on other races or people. You will have the power to meet your own needs.

Minorities have the human right to carry out their own educational systems or activities. Parents have the right to choose the kind of education they want to give their children, along with the institutions of their choosing that teach about their religion, mother tongue, history, morals, cultural traditions, and heritage. Parents have the right to choose other than public schools. Minorities can create educational institutions, private and public schools, online schools, tutors' associations, and private homeschool associations to educate their children. It is a human right! And the State or Country you live in must provide funding, especially if you pay school taxes.

Today, in the year 2023, we see White Americans complaining and changing the educational material taught in schools and kicking out Black history or history that is offensive to white children. In some parts of the country, they are closing down school libraries or taking out books with the subject matter of critical race theory or Black history. White people have the human rights to have their children educated in the manner that they want.

SO DO WE AFRODESCENDANT PEOPLE![4]

Some information on Childrens Human Rights to +education [5]

---

[4] Remember, our languages, names, history, and way of life were taken from our forefathers. Teach a man to fish, and he can feed himself for life. Give a man a fish, and he will come back for food, and then you can get him to work for you for life. It's time to unite all Black people at a single platform to help them become self-sufficient and able to provide for themselves.

[5] Universal Declaration of Human Rights (1948) Article 26.3
Convention Against Discrimination in Education (CADE) Provisions Articles 5
(b) (c)International Covenant on Economic, Social and Cultural Rights (ICEESCR) Article 13.33
Convention of the Rights of the Child (CRC) Article 29
International Covenant on Civil and Political Rights (ICCPR) Article 18.4
UNCRC 2009, Para 60ILO Indigenous and Tribal Peoples Convention C169, Article 27
Children's Rights to Mother-Tongue Education in a Multilingual World: www.unesco.org/en/right-education

Chapter 3: Way Of Life

The US administration has not only wiped out many American Indians from the face of the Earth but also deprived them of their sociocultural rights through several policies. The indigenous culture of America has been fundamentally crushed, and the inter-generational inheritance of indigenous lives is under severe threat. The Native Americans are fighting for their way of life and culture. They are filing petitions at different national and international forum, including the United Nations, to get them acknowledged and protect their territory.

Many Native Americans and supporters of Native American rights claim that the US Federal Government has failed to recognize the sovereignty of Native Americans. It has been criticized for trying to unduly govern the Native American people and treat them with suspicion and discrimination as they do Afrodescendant people. According to some advocates, true respect for Native American sovereignty will be held through dealing with the Native American people like any other sovereign nation.[6] The Jewish people in the State of Israel have

---

[66] (2019, January 31). *Native Americans today*. Norwegian Digital Learning era.
https://ndla.no/en/subject:1:4ad7fe49-b14a-4caf-8e19-ad402d1e2ce6/topic:1:b9b98bf8-787d-4d25-a0c6-37c725050502/topic:1:e3bbd497-8bb6-4654-a970-9106cd69e178/resource:1:6203

their own culture, which they have made known to the world. Moreover, their culture and traditions are respected by the entire world. They have their state, Israel, to protect all Jews. The Native American or Aboriginal Indian people have a territory, but unlike the state of Israel, they do not have a military that can protect them. But, despite not having a military, they are still fighting tooth and nail to protect their rights. They have taken to the streets to protest and petition the US government. In addition, they have reached out to the United Nations to raise their voice against violating their human rights. They want to be united as a nation that governs itself, as the Afrodescendant people need to do.

The American government deprived the Native Americans and Afrodescendant people of their cultural rights, which is why they could not create a functioning economy for themselves. This is because culture and traditions are part of an economy; without these, no economy can thrive. The Native Americans and ancestors of Afrodescendant people were forced to follow the traditions of the Caucasians ever since they were enslaved. From their eating habits to revering family values, the Native Americans were forced to adopt everything from the Caucasian Americans. In this modern day and age, they still hold on to Caucasian values and traditions instead of their own. In the case of the Afrodescendant people, they have no idea what tribes they are from and what languages and traditions they have. In the case of Native Americans, their culture is not being taught in schools, but at least they have their culture. However, in the case of the Afrodescendant people, their entire heritage, culture, language, and names that would connect us to our tribes and traditions have been wiped out entirely from our lives.

The Caucasian Americans did everything they could to destroy the Native Americans' sense of community and identity as a tribe. To achieve their sinister objectives, they deprived them of their language, education, religion, and culture and enforced a slew of discriminatory policies over the period. Even their history was kept hidden, as discussed in the previous chapter. According to Rebecca Nagle, an American activist, public speaker, and writer, information about Native Americans has been systematically removed from popular culture and mainstream media.

A report by the National Indian Education Association reveals that 87% of state-level US history textbooks do not mention the post-1900 history of indigenous people. In addition, the Smithsonian Institution claims that things taught about Native Americans in American schools are replete with incorrect information. They fail to depict the real picture of the miseries inflicted on indigenous people and Afrodescendants. The American education system does not enlighten students about their past, which is also a psychological warfare tactic.

The Native Americans have been severely neglected and disrespected by discriminatory actions and policies at the hands of the white people. This difference can be seen in the fact that the average non-native American citizen has not heard about the rain dances, war paint, and war whoops. However, they know nothing about Native American culture and politics. Through the idea of 'kill the Indian, save the man,' the United States deprived the children of the Native Americans of the right to speak their native language, wear their traditional clothes, and carry out their traditional customs and cultural activities. In this way, their language, culture, and identity were erased through cultural genocide (ethnocide). This is the same thing that happened to Afrodescendants' ancestors who were captured and enslaved. These practices were not banned until 1978, when the Indian Child Welfare Act was passed. In this act, it was acknowledged that the breakup of Indian families was caused by giving Indian children to non-Indian families.

From the 1870s to the late 1920s, the US government forcibly imposed English and Christian education on Indian children. Moreover, because of the policy of 'Forced Foster Care,' children were forcibly placed in the care of White Colonizers, which denied them their cultural identity. There were even cases of Indian children getting kidnapped and forced to attend school. The system of American Indian boarding schools caused irreparable damage, especially to Native American youth and children. In these boarding schools,   American Indian children's braids, a symbol of courage, were cut off. This is seen in the school system policies today with the braids and dreadlocks among Afrodescendant children.

Moreover, their traditional clothing was banned, and they were strictly prohibited from speaking their mother tongue. Violators would then suffer from physical and sexual abuse. Similar to Afrodescendants, many Native Americans felt it was difficult for them to preserve traditional activities and promote their culture, which left them confused about their own cultural identity. Due to these practices, Indian children suffered greatly at school; some even died from abuse, disease, and starvation, that we are seeing with Afrodescendant children today.

Even today, they steal the music and ratings that the indigenous people achieve. They become billionaires through the music created by Afrodescendants. Moreover, they exploit their athletic abilities, creativity, inventions, mental intellectual property, and hard labor. All of these are used to maintain another man's way of life. This is also a psychological warfare tactic, which is used against all the original people in a negative sense.

In a recent legal case, a school in Texas was found guilty of discriminating against a Black student due to his hairstyle. The verdict of the judicial ruling has made the legal situation even more terrible. Shockingly, the court deemed the school's decision appropriate per the disciplinary measures taken. Darryl George, a high school student in his third year, has been either assigned in-school suspension at Barbers Hill High School in Mont Belvieu or enrolled in an external disciplinary program throughout most of the academic year. This realization highlights numerous discriminatory hindrances that Afrodescendants frequently encounter in institutions. The entire experience of the student was a graphic portrayal of how discrimination and injustices are deeply entrenched in our social system, with the core of it being the oppression of Black communities. Such incidents create a pressing need to redesign systems that address racial issues and uphold values, principles of inclusivity, and equity standards for all to enjoy.

Other countries notice this kind of injustice and realize that all of this is wrong. The United States government does not favor the unity of

Afrodescendants or Native Americans. Moreover, they use every device, such as media and music, to portray a negative image of the Native Americans and Afrodescendants. The media portrays them as violent people who cannot get along with the civilized world. They try to paint a negative picture of them in front of the world. This is done so that the Afrodescendants and Native Americans follow the American way of life and do not aim for self-determination. To defend the unjust actions of the US government, some American scholars in the 19th century portrayed original peoples as savage, evil, and inferior people. It was quoted by Francis Parkman, a renowned American historian in that period, that the American Indian "will not learn the arts of civilization, and he and his forest must perish together."

In addition to this, another famous American historian, George Bancroft, claimed that the Native Americans were "inferior in reason and moral qualities" as compared to the whites. He even discriminated racially against the Indians by saying, "Nor is this inferiority simply attached to the individual; it is connected with the organization and is characteristic of the race." They have had the same perceptions about Afrodescendants as well.

Over the years, the US government has deprived the Indian tribes of their right to self-governance. American Indians used to live in tribal units, which were their source of strength and moral support. The US government purposely eradicated the tribal system and integrated (forced-assimilation) the Indians into the white society with a completely different way of life. Indians became economically impoverished as they could not find jobs or make a living. Because of this, they experienced deep mental distress under this new way of life.

The Cherokee tribes were thriving in all aspects in the 19th century compared to the whites. However, their tribal system and right to self-governance were challenged by the US government. Due to this, the economic status of the Cherokee community deteriorated. Furthermore, the government tried to abolish Indian reservations through land distribution to disintegrate their tribes eventually. One example of this is the Dawes Act, enacted in 1887. This act authorized the US president to dissolve Indian reservations and abolish tribal land ownership in the Indian reservations. This disintegrated the American Indian communities. The Sun Dance was considered to be the highest form of tribal unity, but it was regarded as 'heresy' and thus banned. Furthermore, most of the land in the Indian reservations was transferred to the white people through auctions.[7]

---

[7] (2022). The American Genocide of the Indians—Historical Facts and Real Evidence. *Ministry of Foreign Affairs, the Peoples' Republic of China.* https://www.fmprc.gov.cn/mfa_eng/wjdt_665385/2649_665393/2022 03/t20220302_10647120.html\

The Afrodescendants and Native Americans must stop begging the US government (rich man's table) to take care of them. The US government did not stop the Jews from seeking self-determination in 1948, the Jews got their state. Moreover, they got reparations from all countries involved in the Holocaust. If they can fight for human rights and get reparations and a country of their own, the Afrodescendants can also do this. The Native Americans deserve the same life as the people of the State of Israel, but they did not get reparations like the Jews did. They were tricked out of statehood and were marginalized through the reservation system, which was introduced to keep Native Americans off lands that white Americans wished to settle. Jewish culture is respected in the world as their human rights to govern and lead their lives themselves. In a similar vein, the Native Americans and Afrodescendants must provide their people with liberty, just like the people of the Jewish state of Israel enjoy with absolute freedom and autonomy. And with that, both Native Americans and Afrodescendants will be able to have freedom, justice, and equality. The US government must be ready to shun its hypocrisy and double standards on human rights issues. Also, it should take into account the severe racial problems and atrocities committed in its own country.[8]

---

[6] Integration is a war tactic that causes ethnocide and forces assimilation. You think you have freedom and quality, but you are losing your identity by integrating into their community, building their society, their way of life as your community and way of life is killed off through political cleansing and social engineering warfare. Psychological war tactics negatively impact your way of life and your communities.

Chapter 4: Black Leaders And Why We Must Study Them

The Afrodescendants have been marginalized, and their culture has been relegated. On the other hand, the Jewish culture has thrived, and they have received full reparations based on a lie that their homeland was Palestine, saying they are the people mentioned in Gen 15: 13-15. It is important to note that these people were never enslaved in Egypt, despite claims made by Latin and Greek philosophers who visited the region but failed to mention any evidence of slavery. In Egypt's records, there is no history of Jews enslaved, but in the USA's history, you find records of Black people enslaved and afflicted for a period of 400 years.

Native Americans have sought self-determination and received reparations. However, their government or society still operates under the control of others, denying them complete reparations and total control over their rights to self-determination. In contrast, Jews and Israelis fought for reparations and self-determination in the United Nations and emerged victorious.

Afrodescendant people are at a crossroads, and their future remains uncertain. They do not have a territory to govern themselves, mainly because of some of their leaders have made incorrect choices, because of the tricks and overwhelming political power of the U.S. government. Examining past and present leaders and their influence on the community is crucial. Unfortunately, some Black people follow leaders of Caucasian origin, or Black handpicked leaders by the United States or European governments.

In marked contrast, many other nations do not allow outsiders to choose their leaders or speak on their behalf. Allowing others to represent or nominate their leadership is a means of controlling them and steering them toward a path that benefits their enemies rather than themselves. Consequently, it is essential to choose leaders wisely today.

To better understand what makes an honest leader, one must educate themselves about past leaders carefully. One way to consider is how leaders receive their money and spend it.

A leader must be an exemplary role model and work toward self-determination, providing guidance and support to elevate his people. A strong leader raises his voice for his community's independence, encouraging the formation of a single nation. If a leader suggests integration and not self-determination, being economically independent in a society of their own, it is a sign that they are not a good leader. A leader must inspire justice, freedom, and equality and empower the community to take decisive actions to achieve autonomy. To gain a comprehensive understanding, one must study the great leaders to gain wisdom and insights from their actions. It is essential to comprehend how they achieved their goals, their level of success, and why they acted in certain ways. The current conditions can be attributed to past experiences, making it necessary to study our forefathers and their unifying efforts. It is essential to identify methods that can be emulated. Also, it is equally important to understand why they failed to develop and benefit the community wholeheartedly.

When it comes to studying the most impactful figures in history, such Black leaders as the Honorable Elijah Muhammad, Noble Drew Ali, Marcus Garvey, Ben Ammi Ben-Israel, Gaspar Yanga, Che, Vicente Guerrero, Toussaint Louverture, Huey P. Newton, Carlotta of Cuba, Queen Mother Moore, Dr. Khalid Muhammad, Muhammad Ali and Bobby Seale, Dr. King, there are many more names, this is just a few.

From 1865 to the 2000s, several Black organizations were established to aid Black people. Organizations, such as the Universal Negro Improvement Association, the Moorish Science Temple of America, the African Community League, the Black Panther Party, the National Negro Business League, the National Black United Front, and specially Lost Found Nation of Islam, Black Urban League, Pan Africa, all played an instrumental role in empowering the Black community by taking business initiatives and building industries, e.g., newspapers, farms, grocery stores, cargo ships, manufacturing plants, import and export companies, Wood's Directory, fleets of airplanes, the Negro Motorist Green Book, and many more.

These organizations enabled Black people to work toward self-determination as a people. We should join these types of organizations. However, these organizations were constantly attacked by the United States' local city governments and the federal government. Some organizations were destroyed, and some of their leaders were imprisoned, killed, or exiled. Some organizations were destroyed after the death of their leaders, and fake leaders took over, changing the organization's original mission from self-determination to assimilation into the white society's way of life.

Studying Black leaders who shaped many organizations and adopted and promoted their ideologies based on equality, mutual respect, freedom and social justice is vital. Similar to past leaders as mentioned earlier in this chapter, it is necessary to know about the present-day leaders such as Honorable Silis Muhammad, Minister Louis Farrakhan, Prof James Small, Conrad Worrill, Ben

Israel, and Queen Misshaki Muhammad (Harriett Abubakr Esq). They offer valuable lessons to teach us about self-determination and how to build a nation for our people.

Through studying leaders of Black organizations, one can learn about their accomplishments, the methods they employed, and the obstacles they faced. This knowledge can empower the Black community to become autonomous and self-determined.

Self-determination is the ability to make decisions and choices based on one's values, beliefs, and preferences without being unduly influenced or controlled by external forces or factors. It is a fundamental human right recognized and protected by various international laws and treaties.

It can apply to various aspects of life, including cultural, political, social, and economic spheres. For example, self-determination may refer to a group's right to determine its political status, practice and preserve its culture, or control its resources.

At the individual level, self-determination is often associated with autonomy, independence, and empowerment. It is important for personal growth and well-being, as it allows individuals to pursue their goals and aspirations and take responsibility for their lives. Do the Afrodescendant people have the freedom to exercise this right without any interference, or are they just denied it? It is a vital aspect of human freedom and dignity and is important in promoting human rights and governance that revolves around the people's will and social justice.

Self-determination is a right and principle that holds a deeper significance for such marginalized communities as the Afrodescendants. Historically, the Afrodescendants have been subjected to oppressive systems that deny them the agency and autonomy to make decisions for themselves as a people. Therefore, self-determination for the Afrodescendants means more than the ability to make individual choices; it means the ability to collectively assert their interests and rights as a nation of people.

Moreover, it also involves the recognition of cultural diversity and the right to preserve and practice one's own culture. For Afrodescendants, this means the right to celebrate their cultural heritages, languages, and traditions without fear of discrimination or suppression. It also alludes to having a say in the governance and management of their communities without external interference or exploitation.

In terms of economic self-determination, Afrodescendants must have the opportunity to equally participate and benefit from economic development that is sustainable and equitable. This includes access to resources and employment and entrepreneurship opportunities, which can help reduce poverty and inequality within our community. Unfortunately, European governments have stopped such initiatives meant for the betterment and socioeconomic uplift of the Black communities.

In essence, self-determination is a transformative process that empowers Afrodescendants to challenge the status quo and create a higher civilization more just and equitable society for ourselves. By advocating for self-determination! We Afrodescendants can assert our rights and reclaim our agency, leading to greater socioeconomic status, which we create freedom, justice and equality for ourselves in our own society.[9]

---

[9] Know one give you freedom, justice, or equality, you given it to yourself. Fight for it on all levels, economically, legally, spiritually, mentally, politically and physically when necessary. The instrument you must use is a government.

Chapter 5: Black Men Must Provide

The future of Afrodescendants rests upon our collective ability to address social inequalities, promote economic empowerment, and preserve our cultural legacy. We can forge a more equitable and inclusive society by dismantling systemic [10]forced assimilation and embracing independency. Nurturing an environment where Afrodescendants can thrive and contribute their invaluable contributions is of paramount importance. Proactive measures are indispensable in creating a brighter future for Afrodescendants and all other original people of different cultures, regardless of their racial or ethnic backgrounds. Let us embark on this journey together, steering toward a future where Afrodescendant people can flourish, fulfill, and unleash their true potential.

When examining the lives of two extraordinary Black leaders, Malcolm X, and Martin Luther King Jr., it becomes evident that they shared a common aspiration for justice, freedom, and equality for Black people. However, their approaches and ideologies diverged significantly. While one embraced non-

---

[10] Forced Assimilation has often been accompanied by significant social, cultural, psychological, and education, to impact ethic groups to assimilate into the dominant culture to suppressing and banning history, languages and cultures. Relocating ethnic groups into dominant groups by laws and policies like integration law.

violence and advocated for nonviolence when faced with adversity, preferring to refrain from retaliation in the fight for civil rights, the other championed human rights and emphasized the need to protect oneself, one's family, and the Black community through self-defense rather than aggression.

Despite their contrasting ideologies, Malcolm X and Martin Luther King Jr. were motivated by their visions of a better future for Black people. They recognized the significance of unity and engaged in discussions to find ways to work toward a shared goal. They met, trying to work together to come up with the best plan to create a powerful movement with their different ideologies. Malcolm told Martin that they wanted human rights; thus, Martin should take civil rights to a human rights issue. During this time, Martin Luther King met with the Honorable Elijah Muhammad, which caused a shift in the focus of his speeches toward human rights. He began passionately speaking about the need to claim what is rightfully owed to the Black community, Black colleges, and grants for land, which is drawing parallels to reparations in today's society.

Martin Luther King's encounter with Elijah Muhammad marked a turning point in his advocacy. The concept of reparations became a central theme in his speeches, aligning with Malcolm X's emphasis on the inherent rights of Black people. By calling for a "check," Martin Luther King metaphorically alluded to the overdue debt owed to the Afrodescendant community—an acknowledgment of the historical injustices they endured. It was a call for societal restitution and an attempt to rectify the systemic disadvantages that burdened Black people. In today's context, reparations have gained significant momentum to address historical injustices and systemic racism. The idea behind reparations is to provide finances to inquire a large land mass to build cities with all the necessary tools and equipment to accomplish this and compensate those Afrodescendant communities who have suffered disenfranchisement and oppression of human rights. It aims to acknowledge the enduring side effects of slavery and discrimination on the descendants of those who endured these oppressive systems.

Both Malcolm X and Martin Luther King recognized the importance of reparations in their unique ways. Malcolm X's emphasis on economic empowerment, not integrating, and self-defense stemmed from a desire to protect Black communities from further harm because the U.S. Police Departments have been using terrorist tactics to terrorize Afrodescendant communities. A police officer kills a Blackman. You see it on a video, but that officer never goes to jail. These are psychological terrorist tactics. Martin Luther King's call for reparations sought to address the economic and social disparities that had plagued the Black community for generations. Despite their differing approaches, they understood that systemic change could only achieve freedom, justice, and equality. Their shared stance on the need for reparations marked a pivotal moment in the civil rights movement, demonstrating the power of collaboration and the potential for different ideologies to converge toward a common goal. By combining their perspectives, Malcolm X and Martin Luther King created a more nuanced and comprehensive narrative for the fight against racial injustice. They recognized that they could pursue their shared objectives through different means, yet their ultimate purpose remained unchanged —to secure a brighter future for their people.

Malcolm X and Martin Luther King may have initially championed divergent ideologies, focusing on non-violence, human rights, and self-defense. However, they both possessed a profound commitment to the advancement of Black people and the pursuit of justice. Their collaboration and shared emphasis on reparations demonstrated that different approaches could converge to address systemic racism and bring about meaningful change. Their united front exemplified the power of unity and served as a testament to the enduring legacy of their respective visions.

Afrodescendant men find themselves in a crucial moment in history. They reflect on the atrocities of their past—the deceits, falsehoods, and schemes imposed upon us by government programs and policies that promised progress but yielded little. It is time to shift our focus to the future, envision the world we desire, and take the necessary steps to shape it. At this juncture, we stand at the crossroads, confronted with a choice: continue along the path we have tread for far too long, accepting the status quo and relying on the benevolence of others, or forge a new path toward self-determination. The latter is the path we must pursue.

It is time to define what that path looks like for ourselves, to chart a course toward a society where we can live harmoniously among ourselves first, then with others.

Presently, we find ourselves immersed in a society where we played a significant role in shaping it. Yet, the white people within this society are reaping the benefits. At the same time, we languish at the bottom, pleading for a seat at the table by sending Black House representatives and Black senators to the affluent white man's table. The United States government and its programs metaphorically represent this table and the Black representatives begging in Congress for grants, programs, and bills to protect Black people (like the HR40 Bill, the George Floyd Bill, the Civil

Rights Bill, and the Voting Rights Bill). Unfortunately, the programs they offer us, the Afrodescendants, are far from helpful, and these bills are crumbs off the table when signed into law, like the Juneteenth Holiday. How is it, and what is it doing to help us, the Afrodescendants, move toward self-determination and become independent people? Our ancestors were brought to America as slaves to work, and now we are doing the same, but working for the white society and paying taxes out of our low wages. Do we really have representation despite this taxation? The laws were created in this country to protect and improve the Caucasian's way of life. These laws are amended over time to ensure they stay in power and are saved.

We are forced to beg and march for equality but still don't get freedom or liberty. Remember what President Lincoln said in his address on Colonization to the committee of colored men on August 15, 1862. This is what he said, "Perhaps you have long been free, or all your lives. Your race are suffering, in my judgment, the greatest wrong inflicted on any people. But even when you cease to be slaves, you are yet far removed from being placed on an equality with the white race. You are cut off from many of the advantages which the other race enjoy. The aspiration of men is to enjoy equality with the best when free, but on this broad continent, not a single man of your race is made the equal of a single man of ours. Go where you are treated the best, and the ban is still upon you. I do not propose to discuss this, but to present it as a fact with which we have to deal. I cannot alter it if I would.."

So, Lincoln said for you to get out of the USA, to create your own colony or government, and it is a ban that is still imposed on you today. We solicit the Congress for bills that die on the floor or, if passed, are a diluted version of itself crumbs off the table.

However, we are still trapped in the cycle of dependence. These programs fail to empower us as individuals striving for self-determination. We must establish a government instead of relying on another government for our well-being. Creating a government tailored to our needs is the path to reclaiming our autonomy and freedom. We must design programs and initiatives that uplift us and address our unique challenges.

Moreover, establishing a government will allow us to shape a destiny according to our aspirations and world view values. We can develop policies prioritizing education, entrepreneurship, and equal opportunities for all community members. By governing ourselves, Afrodescendants can foster an environment where self-determination and self-reliance flourish.

We can transcend this predicament first and have the intellect, resilience, and a long history of accomplishments that validate our value. We are capable of being productive members of our own society, assuming positions of leadership and authority. We can be mayors, governors, senators, Congress members, and even presidents in our society. We have what it takes to govern ourselves and shape our destinies. The Blackman's and women's intellectual capacity knows no limits. We have brilliant professional architects, engineers, biologists, mathematicians, mechanics, physicians, pharmacists, dentists, computer programmers, lawyers, and others. In fact, whatever occupation it is, we have full knowledge of it. The Afrodescendants possess the knowledge and skills to harness the planet's resources, transforming raw materials into remarkable inventions. It is time to cast off the chains of the past and liberate ourselves from the constraints imposed upon us. We must foster a sense of unity and purpose among ourselves, constructing bridges and nurturing relationships that transcend superficial disparities. In doing so, we shall harness our collective strength and work toward a shared vision. Throughout history, remarkable individuals like George Washington Carver have left an impact on the world that cannot be overstated. Although many influential figures remain unfamiliar to the general public, our contributions have left an indelible mark on society. Whether through scientific discoveries, artistic achievements, or social advancements, these unsung heroes have shaped the very fabric of the existence of human beings. Their efforts have paved the way for progress, innovation, and a better future. Their legacies testify to the power of human ingenuity and the profound influence one person can have on history.

To secure a prosperous future for our offspring, Afrodescendants must adopt a long-term perspective that empowers our children to forge their destinies. We dwell within a societal framework shaped by our predecessors, necessitating a shift toward self-determination. However, Afrodescendants are a highly educated populace, e.g., look at our forefathers in the 1800s and early 1900s. Their skill sets encompass various professions, such as CEOs of insurance companies, banks, generals, sea captains, and scientists, and have companies and manufacturing units. Through their ingenuity, they have contributed significantly to the world's advancements. Their innovative minds have contributed to countless inventions, which are utilized globally. For instance, the visible impact of the traffic signal, which Garret Morgan, an esteemed inventor, made possible. Numerous other inventors have similarly made noteworthy contributions. Notably, the creation of blood plasma, widely used in medical procedures, is credited to a Blackman. Afrodescendants can construct a society that caters to the needs of the intelligence and expertise of their fellow individuals. However, we must embark on a path of self-determination, as historically, our leaders have tended to assimilate into existing societies rather than establish their own government or nation. By forging this approach, we can create a community that fully embraces our potential and secures our collective future. Education will serve as their bedrock, empowering future generations with knowledge and skills that enable them to thrive in any chosen field. It is high time to turn off this road of integration and civil rights since it has not given us as a people freedom, justice, or equality in the Americas, and we are still fighting in 2023. So, turn on the road to human rights and independence and be self-determined.

How? By providing Food, Clothes, and Shelter. We must get to the core of family unity and teach economics, as this is the state of mind we must have. If we are the only ones farming the food that feeds our people, then we know the food is healthy to eat. We manufacture the clothes so we know it is not toxic to wear. We build the homes and buildings so our children can see a society that is theirs and for themselves.

We must cultivate a culture of entrepreneurship, promoting innovation and economic autonomy. By establishing businesses, jobs, and opportunities within our communities, we can elevate ourselves and pave the way for prosperity. Rather than seeking revenge or fostering division, we should strive for justice, equality, and fair representation. Through our achievements, we will dismantle the obstacles in our path and demand recognition for their contributions. Our success will testify to our determination, resilience, and unwavering spirit.

The road ahead may present challenges, but the potential for a brighter future beckons us. We must seize this opportunity and transform our collective dreams into reality. By envisioning a society founded on freedom, justice, and equality, and mutual respect, a world can be created where every Afrodescendant can thrive, regardless of the obstacles they have encountered in the past.

We Afrodescendants should embark on this journey toward self-determination, drawing inspiration from our shared history and the legacies of those who preceded us. Together, we can shape a future that surpasses the limitations imposed upon us, where our potential knows no bounds. It is time for us to take charge of our destiny and forge a society that celebrates and uplifts every Afrodescendant, leaving a legacy that will inspire future generations.

In today's world, economic empowerment plays a crucial role in community development, making it essential for the Afrodescendant community to unite economically. By recognizing the significance of economic strength, we can break free from the cycle of financial disparity. This narrative will delve into prioritizing economic unity, promoting our culture, and supporting our businesses. Economic unity is the cornerstone for building a prosperous future. We can stimulate economic growth and create a self-sustaining cycle by directing our spending power within our community. It is imperative to prioritize supporting Black-owned businesses, entrepreneurs, and professionals. By doing so, we ensure that the money circulates within our community, creating opportunities for economic advancement, job creation, and the overall improvement of our neighborhoods.

Our culture is rich, diverse, and unique; we must promote and profit from it. Others often appropriate our culture and profit from it while we receive mere pennies in return. By reclaiming the promotion of our traditions, arts, music, and heritage, we preserve our cultural identity and generate revenue within our community. By becoming the curators and entrepreneurs of our culture, we can ensure that the economic benefits stay within our community, helping us thrive and flourish.

Education and instilling a sense of community pride within our youth are essential for fostering economic unity. We must teach our children the importance of supporting their community and businesses. They need to understand that it is not just about finding the cheapest option; it is about investing in their people and the future of their community. By imparting this wisdom, we empower our children to become successful entrepreneurs, business owners, and professionals who contribute to our community's economic growth and sustainability. Through unity and economic empowerment, we can build a community that thrives economically, celebrates its unique heritage, and uplifts its people, ensuring a brighter and more prosperous future for all.

After generations of oppression and marginalization, the Afrodescendant men must plan for their family's future. This entails assuming responsibility for their economic, spiritual, physical, emotional, educational, and cultural well-being. Through deliberate teaching and training, these values and traditions must be imparted to the children until they master and implement them within the family unit. When replicated in each household, such efforts fortify the community, laying the foundation for essential establishments like restaurants, bakeries, schools, and businesses that sustain and uplift the community. This process also shapes the mindset and leadership qualities of individuals within the community, ultimately strengthening it. As the community flourishes, this paradigm spreads throughout the nation, culminating in the establishment of self-governance and institutions designed to safeguard our way of life and protect the inherent rights of our people.

Afrodescendant men must shift their mindset and aspire to operate globally. Having others represent us is no longer acceptable, as their portrayals often do not align with our true identity and aspirations. We must be in the U.N. and the world congregation to assert our narratives and worldviews that revolve around such universal values as freedom, justice, equality, truth, and righteousness. Then, we can be like the mustard seed in the garden.

We need to reclaim our agency and actively participate in shaping the image we project to the world. By doing so, we can dismantle stereotypes and present an accurate reflection of our diverse and vibrant community. It is crucial to develop and strengthen our institutions. These institutions should mirror the structures and functions of other governments, providing support and protection for our society. The principles of self-determination, equity, and justice should drive them. By establishing these institutions, we can empower ourselves and create a solid foundation for our community to thrive.

Moreover, we must recognize the significance of our God-given rights and safeguard them through our self-governance. It is through embracing our heritage and understanding the value of our rights that we can build a society that upholds and respects the dignity of every individual. By taking control of our destiny, we ensure that future generations can enjoy the fruits of our labor and live in a world that cherishes their identity and rights.

In essence, an Afrodescendant man is profoundly responsible for planning for his family's future with economic stability, spiritual growth, physical well-being, emotional support, educational enrichment, and cultural preservation. This commitment extends to the broader community, creating a solid foundation for essential institutions and empowering individuals to become leaders. As we transcend the community level, our collective efforts pave the way for a self-governing nation that protects our way of life and upholds our inherent rights. It is time for Afrodescendant men to rise, reclaim our narratives, and actively participate in shaping the world's perception of our community.

Chapter 6: Unbreakable Bond

Blackman! We must understand that our forefathers were brought here to work and bring prosperity to America. They were brought here before the Revolutionary War. Do you know why we fought in that war?

When the Constitution of America was being formed, we were helping them fight the British. We have been through all this, yet the Constitution of America doesn't regard us as humans. And after they won the war, they kept us in slavery and also legalized it throughout every state. When you read history, you will see no Blackman or woman was helping write the Constitution of America. To top it off, there was no representation there to speak for our needs.

Today, the descendants of the enslaved people who fought and lost their lives in these wars in the past and now believe the Constitution protects them. No, that is simply untrue. You are barely considered a human being in it.

After the Civil War, the 13th Amendment came about, but when you read it, you realize it just says 'no slavery in the US.' It leaves us in limbo with no rights. After the Civil War, Black people wanted to create a civil rights bill that was never passed in the late 1800s. But if you are a citizen of America, like they say, the Bill of Rights gives you all inalienable rights. We,

Afrodescendants, are not protected by the Bill of Rights in the U.S. Constitution. The Civil Rights Act and the Voting Rights Act of the 1860s were significant improvements to the rights of Black people , but the Voting Rights Act must be signed every 25 years to stay in effect. However, they underscore the ongoing necessity for unity and self-reliance within the Black community. We, Afrodescendant Blackman, must focus on cultivating an unwavering bond among each other, one grounded in respect, trust, loyalty, and honesty. This holds the key to enabling the Black community to govern itself, forge opportunities, and construct a more promising future. The central focus should be empowering the community to collaborate harmoniously, rely on one another, and seize command of their fate. It is up to us, the Afrodescendant Blackman, to build the unshakable bond within our people that even the wind cannot get between us. We shall not break the peace among us.

We shall not let anyone inside or outside divide us because of our differences. We shall use all possibilities to bring peace, brotherhood, and respect among us, the Afrodescendant Black men. Then our women and children shall live safely because we will live in a society that promotes freedom, justice, equality, truth, and righteousness. This will bring peace. We, the Black men, must cling to this bond and never forget it!

Chapter 7: Conclusion

In this fast-paced economic world, not only do Afrodescendants still face racism from white folks, but also lack cultural rights and educational and employment opportunities. The majority of Afrodescendants are either unemployed or receive one-third of what their white coworkers make. This leads to a domino effect where less income turns into fewer savings, and less money leads to an unhealthy lifestyle. The USA is having a hard time employing white people today. This is why they repealed affirmative action.

This inequality is also evident in the educational system due to the economic conditions. White supremacists and politicians pass laws that negatively affect the well-being of Afrodescendants and lead them to poverty and uncertainty. Now, these laws and policies have severely affected the education of young Black individuals, where Black students lag behind their white peers. Their education is hindered by the way they are stereotyped.

The roots of the wide socioeconomic disparities that Afrodescendant Americans face today can be traced back to slavery. Slavery was a system of forced labor in the United States before the Civil War. Under this system, the ancestors of Afrodescendants were considered property and were subjected to brutal treatment, including physical and sexual abuse, lack of medical care, and limited educational opportunities. The scars of slavery are apparent in the present system as well. It's in the form of mass imprisonment, police violence, and a lack of educational opportunities for Afrodescendants.

Education regarding slavery is critical to bridging the racial differences that split the nation. However, the students are not taught the true American history in the schools of America. Educators do not pay heed to teaching about slavery and the misdeeds of white supremacists, and textbooks do not have enough material to make things worse. Therefore, students are ignorant of its significant role in shaping America.

Today, the Caucasian system is becoming successful in influencing the Afrodescendants' way of life. This is because the Afrodescendants have resorted to dependence, some Black people hiding and fearful, leading to a myriad of problems they face today, forgetting their strength as a community. Afrodescendants are in a palingenesis (a concept of re-creation and rebirth)[11] ethnogenesis[12], which can

---

[11] Palingenesis typically refers to the concept of rebirth, regeneration, or renewal. It can refer to the renewal or revival of a society, culture, or individual in various contexts. It often denotes a spiritual or moral rebirth or transformation in philosophical and religious contexts.
[12] Ethnogenesis refers to the process through which a distinct ethnic group forms, often involving the merging or separation of different cultural, linguistic, or historical elements to create a new identity. A new nation can occur through various factors such as migration, social,

be defined as the development and distinct formation of an ethnic group. Hopefully, Afrodescendants will become aware of how they have been exploited and deprived of their way of life, and this realization will help them to evolve into a new nation. The lot of white supremacists damage the Afrodescendants' way of life by keeping them away from their past, abounding in injustice, discrimination, and marginalization. The history that is taught to children nowadays is completely fabricated, and people don't get to learn about the achievements of Black people because they aren't mentioned anywhere in the textbooks. The Europeans mostly take credit for great inventions, disregarding the contributions made by Black people to the field of science and many other knowledge areas.

Most educational institutes in the United States shape the narratives in such a way that the entire history is changed from the word go. The same concocted version of the history is then taught in schools, thus making the students of African descent ignorant of their true history.

History infuses us with feelings of loyalty and pride about our origins, ethnic backdrop, and heritage and helps us to know our past in order to create the future

---

political, and historical events. It involves the formation of a shared identity, language, customs, and traditions among a new group and/or a new nation of people.

in the manner that we envision.

Regrettably, the future of Afrodescendants remains uncertain since they do not have a designated territory as a distinct race or nation, which is mainly owing to the wrong calls made by our leaders. Therefore, examining our past and present leaders and their long-lasting impact and influence on the Black community is equally important. Unfortunately, some Afrodescendants are not genuine leaders and are mostly handpicked and appointed by the Caucasian people, comprising the Americans and the European governments, to represent the Black people, but to no avail.

The US administration has deprived Black people of their sociocultural rights through several discriminatory moves and divisive policies. The indigenous culture of America has severely been exploited, and the Native Americans are fighting to live as per their preferred way of life and culture.

The Afrodescendants and Native Americans must stop going to the rich man's table, which is the United States government. Instead of pleading, they must build their table and put things on it that benefit them.

Self-determination is a fundamental right that holds deeper importance, especially for marginalized communities and groups such as Afrodescendants.

Historically speaking, the Afrodescendants have been exposed to unfair systems denying them the autonomy and agency to make political decisions for themselves. For the Afrodescendants, therefore, the notion of self-determination transcends the ability to make individual choices as it is the final destiny each of us must aim for to lead a life characterized by justice, equality and socioeconomic equilibrium. Moreover, the need for self-determination and free will also necessitates the recognition of cultural diversity and the right to preserve and practice one's own culture and customs without any interference. For Afrodescendants, this leads to the right to celebrate their rich cultural heritage, language, and traditions without fear of discrimination or prejudice. It also refers to the right to have a say in matters of administration and governance without external interference or intrusion from the powers that be.

When it comes to achieving economic autonomy, the Afrodescendants must tap every available opportunity and prospect to take part and benefit from economic development, which is sustainable and equitable. The purpose can be achieved by having absolute access to state resources, employment opportunities, and entrepreneurship. To make this happen, you have to self-govern and build cities on a land, a country of your own on this planet. Reparation can help with this. In doing so, we shall decrease poverty levels and put an end to inequality within our community. In today's fast-paced world, economic empowerment and growth are decisive in community development. Therefore, Afrodescendants can also become financially independent and stand on their own feet by recognizing the significance of economic stability and financial strength.

Afrodescendant men, to be specific, find themselves in a critical moment in history. They reflect on the brutalities of their past imposed upon them by government programs and policies that promised progress but reaped no benefits.

It is time to shift their focus to the future, envision the world they desire, and take the necessary steps to shape it. At this crucial juncture, they stand at a crossroads, confronted with a choice —continue along the path they have tread for far too long, accept the status quo and depend on others, or forge a new path toward self-determination. I firmly believe the latter is the path they must pursue.

Afrodescendants should embark on the self-determination journey, drawing inspiration from their shared history and the legacy of those who preceded them. Together, they can shape a future that surpasses the limitations imposed upon them, where their potential knows no bounds. It is time for them to take charge of their destiny and forge a society that celebrates and uplifts every Afrodescendant, leaving a legacy that will also inspire future generations.

The Afrodescendant man is a valuable asset, but it is important to recognize the importance of the role of women. If a Blackman desires to thrive, he must honor, respect, and protect the Black woman. He should act as a diligent farmer who attentively tends to his crops, being constantly aware of their well-being and needs. It is essential to establish a society that caters to all Afrodescendants' economic, social, mental, and physical needs and desires.

This way, when someone from outside the Afrodescendant society tries to provide or offer something to a Black woman and child, they can confidently refuse, stating that she already has everything she needs within her community. A nation cannot reach its full potential until its women are educated and have equal freedom and equality. The saying goes, "A man cannot raise no higher than his woman."

Furthermore, the Black woman must wholeheartedly support and defend the Blackman, showing support and protecting him, when necessary, legally and relentlessly. While providing much-needed moral and emotional support to the Blackman, she must defend his image in the public's eyes by never uttering a negative word about the Blackman in public. Never side with the open enemy! As grandmother says, "If you don't have something good to say, don't say anything at all" against the

Blackman in public.

End Notes

1. Forced assimilation is the process of compelling individuals or groups to adopt another group's culture, language, customs, and norms through coercion, oppression, outright imposition, or integration. This can occur through policies, laws, or actions imposed by a dominant group onto a marginalized or minority group, often aiming to homogenize society or exert control. Force assimilation can have significant social, psychological, and cultural impacts on the affected populations, leading to feelings of alienation, loss of identity, and resistance. https://law.adelaide.edu.au/ua/media/573/ch4_alr_35-2-pruim.pdf

2. Ethnocide refers to the deliberate and systematic destruction of the culture, language, identity, and way of life of a particular ethnic group. It often involves efforts to eradicate or suppress cultural practices, traditions, and beliefs, as well as the imposition of the dominant culture onto the targeted group. Ethnocide can occur through various means, including forced assimilation, cultural repression, displacement, and violence. It is a form of cultural genocide that aims to eliminate the distinctiveness and autonomy of an ethnic group. What is Ethnocide? https://www.americanbar.org/groups/human_rights/dignity-rights-initiative/ethnocide-project/what-is-ethnocide-/

3. We, the Blackman, must provide for our people first. We have always integrated people, and we always have helped other people even when we are hurting the most. We must stop that and have our best interest at heart, taking care of ourselves first and then helping others.

4. Remember, our languages, names, history, and way of life were taken from our forefathers. Teach a man to fish so that he can feed himself for life. Give a man a fish he will come back for food, and then you can get him to work for you.

5. Universal Declaration of Human Rights (1948) Article 26.3[3]
Convention Against Discrimination in Education (CADE) Provisions Articles 5 (b) (c)
International Covenant on Economic, Social and Cultural Rights (ICEESCR) Article 13.33
Convention of the Rights of the Child (CRC) Article 29
International Covenant on Civil and Political Rights (ICCPR) Article 18.4

6. UNCRC 2009, Para 60 ILO Indigenous and Tribal Peoples Convention C169, Article 27 Children's Rights to Mother-Tongue Education in a Multilingual World: www.unesco.org/en/right-education (2019, January 31). *Native Americans today.* Norwegian Digital Learning era.

7. https://ndla.no/en/subject:1:4ad7fe49-b14a-4caf-8e19-ad402d1e2ce6/topic:1:b9b98bf8-787d-4d25-a0c6-37c725050502/topic:1:e3bbd497-8bb6-4654-a970-9106cd69e178/resource:1:6203

8. (2022). The American Genocide of the Indians—Historical Facts and Real Evidence. *Ministry of Foreign Affairs, the People's Republic of*
China. https://www.fmprc.gov.cn/mfa_eng/wjdt_665385/2649_665393/202203/t20220302_10647120.html\

9. Integration is a war tactic that causes ethnocide and forced assimilation. You think you have freedom and identity, but you are losing your identity by integrating into their community, building their society, their way of life as your community and way of life is killed through political and social engineering and psychological war tactics employed against your way of life and your communities.

10. Palingenesis typically refers to the concept of rebirth, regeneration, or renewal. It can refer to the renewal or revival of a society, culture, or individual in various contexts. It often denotes a spiritual or moral rebirth or transformation in philosophical and religious contexts.

11. Ethnogenesis refers to the process through which a distinct ethnic group forms, often involving the merging or separation of different cultural, linguistic, or historical elements to create a new identity. A new nation can occur through various factors such as migration, social, political, and historical events. It involves the formation of a shared identity, language, customs, and traditions among a new group and/or a new nation of people.